EVERYTHING I NEED TO KNOW I LEARNED AT *VOGUE*

How To Get, Keep, and Succeed In
That First Job After College

MARIA DEVANEY

ISBN: 1512040606
ISBN 13: 9781512040609
Library of Congress Control Number: 2015907327
CreateSpace Independent Publishing Platform
North Charleston, South Carolina

#1: INTRODUCTION

What can you say about a place where champagne was on the weekly office supplies order form? Where a six-foot-long hot-pink feather boa was Monday morning office-wear? A place that had its own voice coach? And where the publisher was the real Mr. Big of *Sex and the City* fame?

What would you call this place? *Vogue.*

Have you ever imagined yourself working for the world's most powerful fashion magazine? I did. But after I landed this impossible-to-get job, I found myself on a wild ride--- one for which I was not initially equipped.

So *Vogue* made me over, from the inside out. And when they were finished I was permanently transformed. I discovered the magazine could take twenty-somethings and turn them into polished professionals, and I know their secrets for doing so.

And here's the best part. It turns out that following *Vogue's* unique formula is critical to success in fashion or any other industry: technology, education, finance, law, medicine, non-profit, you name it.

So if the world were your personal runway, how would you choose to walk it? You would want to be fabulous in the moment, wouldn't you? Here you will find exactly what it takes to pull it off.

#2: ABOUT THIS AUTHOR

Years after her time spent at the magazine, *Vogue* veteran Maria Devaney is keenly aware that these lessons learned once upon a time still enrich every area of her life. This mother of three knows that *Vogue* equipped her to be successful in subsequent positions at *The New York Times* and in her current career too.

But before we move on to share Maria's stories...

#3: WHAT DO *YOU* KNOW ABOUT *VOGUE?*

Vogue gives us breaking news on fashion, beauty, and must-have shopping dictates. But, you knew that.

It also provides unique and of-the-moment insight into politics, health, and cultural movements, all the while giving us the latest in film, music, books, technology, interior design, travel, and food. Interesting? Yes.

What you *now* need to know is that *Vogue* gives us a glimpse into a highly educated and progressive United States mindset, and it provides a unique window into American innovation. It also shapes our collective cultural curiousness in a way that, in this author's opinion, has to date been enormously underestimated. Yes. Wow.

But there's more. Marketers once asked U.S. consumers to name the best-known American brands. *Vogue*, Coke, and Microsoft all made the list. However, to the most sophisticated marketers, *Vogue* stands out, even in this incredibly competitive crowd. U.S. politicians and international figureheads don't trip over one another to partner with Coke or Microsoft when they need to do any or all of the following: tell their personal story, improve their image, or, you know, bridge international relations. Yet, have you noticed how serious power players line up to appear in *Vogue?* Michelle Obama, Laura Bush, Hilary Clinton, and Queen Rania of Jordan are pre-eminent examples of those who understand the profound impact of their close-up. And while advancing other causes, it doesn't hurt that each gets to look fabulous while they're at it--- the result of working with *Vogue's* living legend stable of talent which counts among others Creative Director Grace Coddington, make-up artists like Stephane Marais, and photographers Arthur Elgort and Mario Testino. Awesome, right?

So, together let's look for inspiration from *Vogue*, already at the forefront of fashion, and one might argue, everything else. Here you will learn how *Vogue* sharpens the edges of its individual staffers to magnify its own, and you will discover that this particular place has its own recipe for doing so. To succeed at *Vogue* means mastering how business is done at the very highest levels inside America's elite institutions.

You will also find building blocks for success, taken once upon a time from *Vogue's* hallways, cubicles, and corner offices. This insider's checklist will help you achieve ingenuity, status, style, and substance in your own life so you can channel your very own inner *Vogue*--- and play at your peak in any field.

#4: ELEVATE YOUR IMAGE TO EXTRACT YOURSELF FROM THE MUCK

In buying this book, you have just taken an important step toward improving whatever state you find yourself in at the moment: exhausted by a futile job hunt, beaten up from rejection after rejection in job interviews, wondering why you chose a specific career, abused by an incompetent boss, jousting with a jealous coworker, low pay/long hours, awesome perks/long hours.

I experienced all of the above while working at *Vogue*. There were many days when the relentless pace, the punishing politics, and the overwhelming workload felt like too much, and when I thought my best move might be to quit. Quitting often crossed my mind and seemed, in the moment, like the best way to put myself in control--- before they fired me.

But they didn't fire me. Instead I eventually walked out of my own accord, and permanently better off for the experience.

I see myself as a beneficiary of a most unusual, very formal, and highly desirable education. I finally understand its unique value, and now appreciate that few people get to experience it firsthand. And as it turns out, everything I need to know, I learned at *Vogue*. So let's step inside to see how they do it.

The Lesson: *Vogue* whipped me into shape for the real world and I will tell you how they did it. I will also share with you how I got the job, kept the job, and what I discovered about life. It turns out we can all learn a lot from this particular fashion magazine, bringing entirely new meaning to the power of *Vogue.*

#5: WELCOME TO THE JUDGEMENT ZONE

When you leave college, you will enter into The Judgment Zone. No one will tell you this. I repeat. *No one will tell you this.*

From this moment on, getting the job, doing the job, and succeeding on the job will depend on other people's opinions of you, their assessments, endless evaluations, and unsolicited (and frankly sometimes stupid and useless) advice and input. In other words, your future will depend on what these people whom you will meet decide they think of you. They will notice what you are wearing, they will take note if you don't look them in the eye and firmly shake their hand, and they will privately judge as you tell them about yourself. Yes, brutal.

How much criticism can one person take? Sometimes working at *Vogue* felt like walking on eggshells, where every corner I turned, or cubicle I passed, or ladies room encounter was met by a comment on my hair or my posture, or some backhanded compliment like, "Wow, those shoes must be so *comfy.*" Talk about the ultimate judgment zone! There were no triangular signs posted to warn me about this point of no return, I walked in clueless and completely unprepared. I walked out exactly the opposite.

I witnessed many a remarkable metamorphosis at *Vogue*, including my own. And since there were only about one hundred of us on staff at the time, it seemed impossible to avoid the spotlight of judgment, first as an inductee into the process and then as a contributor among many to the indoctrination of its new arrivals.

There was no playbook or primer filled with insider's information. If such a thing had existed, it would have felt heaven-sent in the moment. Instead, the transformation took place in the form of a very public and painful initiation into *Vogue* as state-of-mind and physical being. While the process was certainly stressful and straining, there was definitely light at the end of the tunnel. As a *Vogue* survivor, I learned that style is always personal and polished, that being super-smart is cool, and that aspiring to the highest levels of organization is only everything.

> **The Lesson: Empower yourself to elevate the impression you make on the world, since from now on people will make snap judgments in your presence. Equip yourself with the skills to pass anyone's assessment of you--- so you too can survive, flourish and have the last laugh.**

#6: REJECTION ISN'T FINAL

Have you been turned down for the dream entry-level position from the even dreamier company? Please know that how you handle this rejection will make the difference between landing that next opportunity, and not.

On my very first visit to *Vogue*, I failed Human Resource's typing test, which immediately disqualified me from meeting anyone who actually worked at the magazine. But it was only after my first rejection that I finally realized how much I really wanted to work there.

So I made a second attempt, and failed HR's typing test *again*.

Rejection #2 hurt. A lot.

I licked my wounds, took stock, and decided I was willing to fight for it. I laid low for a bit (to give HR a rest from my enthusiastic self), and then went back a third time, glutton for punishment that I was.

Round three my interview with HR went so well that they even let me skip the typing test. HR came up with a role for me that day that surpassed my wildest expectations--Merchandising Editor. If I could somehow pass the next grueling round of interviews, I would become the face of *Vogue* to its readers, advertisers, and the press.

In retrospect, I believe HR employed their typing test to instantly end the interview process with someone they had no interest in hiring. So I was relieved to break through this perhaps bizarre but very real barrier.

I made it through multiple rounds of meetings with *Vogue* staffers, and gave a formal presentation, which must have gone reasonably well. It appeared they might hire me, and it felt like too much to hope for.

The last step in the process was to meet *Vogue's* Publisher Ron Galotti and protocol dictated that just prior to that I would be presented to Editor in Chief Anna Wintour. If Anna was reviled by the very sight of me she could--- and would--- end my chances for that reason alone, and by the way this did happen at *Vogue*. However, for some strange reason, I was instructed to skip my meeting with Anna and go straight to see Ron. Even HR was excited for me.

All I needed to do now was walk in and land this job which would become a credential I would permanently possess--- since to work, or to have worked, at *Vogue* is considered to be a mark of distinction.

My interview with Ron Galotti, the real life inspiration for *Sex and the City's* Mr. Big character, took place in his office at 8:30 on a Monday morning. Ron's assistant Renee walked me into his office, and seated us in leather club chairs in a tucked off corner of the room, next to the table which housed his prized humidor. Ron was wearing a showy pin-striped suit, an expensive watch that screamed "notice-me" and there was a lot of product used to get his hair slicked front-to-back just so. He leaned back in his club chair, put his feet up, lit a cigar, and looked at me. He asked if I understood how high profile this (in context rather low level) position would be, and if I understood the amount of travel it would require. I told him I was ready for both. Ron asked if I was prepared to work hard, and I told him I was ready to do so. He blew out a puff of his cigar, sat up, leaned forward and asked, "So, are ya married?" Ron's last question would have set HR's hair on fire, so I kept it under wraps until now. The meeting was over, and I knew I had the job.

My *Vogue* story illustrates that the path to success is often littered with setbacks, and no one is immune to this reality. Remember that rejection is not necessarily final, and the key to success instead lies in how you respond when things don't go your way. The front end of the process forced me to put up with useless typing tests, two rejections, three call-backs, and horribly inappropriate questions. The experience doesn't have to make sense while you are living through it. You just need to know why you are subjecting yourself to its seemingly endless demands.

> **The Lesson: Good things come to those who don't give up. In the meantime, you might become a fantastic typist.**

#7: SUCCESS CAN BE SUPER-SCARY

Do you worry that you have set your sights impossibly high within an industry in which you want to work, and are you secretly afraid that you might be interviewing out of your league? Conversely, does it feel like you are scraping the bottom of the barrel of "opportunities" when it comes to the posts you answer, and the positions for which you pretend to express interest?

We have all felt like that more often than we care to admit. For me, in actually landing this dream job, it was the former that struck a nerve.

When I set my sights on *Vogue*—the Who's Who of power, product, and placement, I wanted that triple threat of association to be mine. But when I actually started the job, I looked around at the chic, shiny, and supremely confident staffers who graced its halls and decided I had been certifiable for thinking I could ever belong there. From the beginning, my career at *Vogue* brought me tears, sleepless nights, and nausea--- and that was on a good day.

I walked into the place day one, privately panicked, and asked myself: *Are the people who work at Vogue simply born ready-to-work there?* I met people who had known "Oscar" (de la Renta) since birth, had spent summers in college assisting (photographer) Bruce Weber, and for whom "Mark and James"

(Badgley Mischka) insisted on making their wedding dress. Inside this insanely exclusive of inner circles, I felt like an outsider, and my imagination ran wild with all of the ways I might fail in front of everyone at *Vogue*, to include of all people Anna Wintour.

Looking back on this trying time, I want to tell my young self that I was hired because I possessed substance and grit. In the moment, I should have spent more time channeling the confidence that *Vogue* ironically already had in me.

The Lesson: Are the shiny chic *Vogue* staffers who possess that air of confidence so unique to this particular place actually *each one of us*, just the new-and-improved variety? Yes. Are these same people, who walked in day one as mere mortals, actively made by *Vogue* into its own image, from the inside out? They are. We each have the potential to transform ourselves into that confident and collected person who appears to have it all together.

#8: WHEN IN ROME

During my first week at *Vogue*, I was invited to what was to be one of many intimate intra-office celebrations to come. We gathered to celebrate each other's birthdays, upcoming weddings, and pending arrivals--- new babies, or new jobs--- with champagne and cupcakes, always at 4:00pm in the *Vogue* Room on Condé Nast's 12th floor at 350 Madison Avenue. In this first week, I found myself attending one of these small-scale celebrations with Anna Wintour as fellow reveler.

Stick thin, and startlingly striking in person, Anna achieved a unique physical presentation that was perplexingly perfect and seemingly unattainable for the rest of us. Her sinewy physique, super straight posture, razor sharp intellect, and individual style made her appear larger than life. Her steely calm added to her overall aura, which always threw everyone around her completely off center.

My instincts told me not to eat a cupcake in front of Anna Wintour--- week one, or ever. And I learned that day that while fabulous fashion people keep champagne on hand for its celebratory sensibilities, they don't actually drink it.

So I put a cupcake on my plate, didn't take a bite, and took the smallest sip of champagne possible as we toasted the birthday boy. I had just passed my first important test at *Vogue*.

> **The Lesson: When in Rome, do as the Romans do. When you find yourself dropped into an unfamiliar environment, mirror the actions of those around you. And do so until you find your own footing within the organization, and earn the credibility to eventually do things differently.**

#9: POWER IS NOT AS IT APPEARS

Only years later do I find it strange that Margit & Helmut, the colorful German couple who owned Condé Nast's lobby newsstand, made a living selling magazines and newspapers to those who ran a magazine and newspaper empire. That should have been my first clue that there was much more than meets the eye with regard to their position in this otherwise glamorous mix.

Si Newhouse presided over Advance Publications, a company he owned lock stock and barrel. Advance Publications owned a larger collection of media holdings, which included among other things a newspaper group, and Condé Nast.

Condé Nast was Si's favorite child in the family, and published magazines that included at the time *Vogue, Vanity Fair, Glamour, GQ, Architectural Digest, Mademoiselle, Gourmet,* and *Self.* Most of these magazines, *Vogue* included, were housed at 350 Madison Avenue in Manhattan. Lesser revenue generating titles, such as *Condé Nast House & Garden* and *Details,* were farmed out to another building located just steps away.

Si, while physically diminutive in size, was otherwise larger than life and sat ensconced somewhere within 350 Madison. He enjoyed blowing a breeze, and every so often a tornado, through his castle and kingdom.

And since his presence in our lives was always felt but he was rarely seen, a Si sighting in the lobby or in an elevator was big news at *Vogue* and was always reported in to our 12th floor offices. Si was the Wizard and his media empire was Oz. Condé Nast was Dorothy, and the Advance newspaper group appeared to be Toto. 350 Madison Avenue was definitely The Emerald City.

As a corporate perk, Condé Nast employees were given every in-house magazine they asked for every month by the company, and for free. Yet assistants, both advertising and editorial, still made multiple visits every day to Margit & Helmut's newsstand, always returning to their individual boss' offices with towering stacks of magazines and newspapers. Transporting these teetering piles back upstairs to their desks, in short skirts and high heels, was hard work.

These buying sprees were an official part of every assistant's job description, and this gathering exercise always included the purchase of one's magazine's competitive titles. So if, for example, you worked at *Vogue*, you and your boss were buying *Harper's Bazaar* (a Hearst publication) to keep a close eye on what they were up to. No matter which magazine you worked for, *The New York Post* was always in the pile for its Page Six gossip column. For the fashion set, obscure titles like *Visionaire*--- which eventually carried a $425 per issue price tag--- were somewhere in the stack. Each Condé Nast magazine had its own house account with Margit & Helmut, and was billed directly by them every month.

Margit was plump, authoritarian, spoke in a thick German accent, and handled all transactions. She favored dreary synthetic pant and top separates in muddy colors, and tragically sensible shoes. Helmut was tall, skinny and bespectacled, and did everything else. Every day, he wore ratty jeans, a t-shirt, and running shoes since he was always on the go.

Margit presided over the cash register and rang up sale after sale, all day every day. Helmut spent his time from dawn until dusk bringing goodness only knows what else (to include fresh juices and candy) to individual Condé Nast offices, since additional orders for delivery could also be called in. When not making his rounds, Helmut re-stocked the shelves and beverage case, just to keep up with the endless demand.

The real value of Margit & Helmut was that they were completely woven into the fabric of daily life at Condé Nast. They knew *everything*, in real time. Either one of them could tell you whose career was looking up, and whose was in a downward spiral--- from entry level positions all the way up to luminary. They knew who was getting a big promotion next week, and who had had their head handed to them six seconds ago. Everyone within the empire fed breaking news into Margit & Helmut all day long. So if you wondered what was cooking behind closed doors at your own magazine, you took the elevator down to see Margit & Helmut for the update.

Since they were the human tickers of who was up and who was down in the organization at any given moment, there were perhaps two no more important people at Condé Nast than Margit & Helmut.

> **Lesson One: Power is not always as it appears. The people who wield true influence within an organization may not be immediately obvious to you. Instead, they could be hiding in plain sight. Pay close attention when you are new to any company and do your best to identify its clandestine information brokers, since absolutely every organization has them. Befriend these people, and make the effort to weave interactions with them into your day.**

> **Lesson Two: Were Margit & Helmut Si Newhouse's personal paid operatives, spies extraordinaire who trafficked in internal information as part of some grand corporate master plan? We don't know. But the savviest at Condé Nast knew to filter communications through these two, and saw them as their personal guardian angels operating from within.**

#10: DUE DILIGENCE DIGS UP THE UNEXPECTED
Still on the subject of Margit & Helmut…

Pity the poor fool who stopped by their newsstand to flip casually through anything without buying it first. Stories made the rounds of Margit's head practically popping off as she shrieked at the top of her lungs and physically assaulted publication flipping perpetrators, while running them out of her prized corner of Condé Nast. Worse, these scenes were always terribly public, since the newsstand sat directly across from the elevator bank which every employee used to go anywhere in the building. News of a Margit blow-up spread like wildfire all over Condé Nast.

I first heard about Margit & Helmut early in the interview process at *Vogue*. During approximately two years, it had taken me several attempts to get this close to an offer from Condé Nast. So for this third round of things, and with an actual shot at a job offer, I left nothing to chance in preparing for my next visit.

I called ahead to some trusted friends who worked in the building to tell them that I was coming to interview with HR *again*, and to remind them of how much I wanted to work at *Vogue*. Everyone gave me the same advice: "When you arrive in the lobby and find yourself with a few minutes to kill, for the love of God, do not visit the newsstand and flip through anything. If you do, horrible things will happen, and your meeting will not go well".

When I worked at *Vogue*, we all gave the exact same advice when anyone called ahead to tell us they were coming to the building for a meeting of any kind.

However, one day a colleague received a call from her college frenemy, who shared that she had an upcoming job interview at Condé Nast. This friend of mine matter-of-factly told her nemesis that when walking into the building "it's best to show interest by flipping through magazines at the lobby newsstand, before going up to HR".

The day and time of the frenemy's visit arrived, and we all sat upstairs on the edge of our seats--- waiting for a report from the lobby of a Margit implosion. And at the appointed hour, news of one, of course, came in. Well-deserved or not, our friend's friend received some serious come-uppance that day. And oh yes, the frenemy did not get the job.

> **The Lesson: Sometimes excellent career advice comes in the most bizarre forms. Only those who did full front-end due diligence, through carefully selected and trustworthy sources, knew to avoid a visit to the newsstand when interviewing at Condé Nast. And when asked for advice, those on the inside knew to administer this little nugget under the heading "critical".**

#11: BED CHECKS WITH MR. BIG

Survival at *Vogue* required adjusting to Publisher Ron Galotti's individual quirks. Ron believed that his direct reports were motivated by "fear and greed" to keep their jobs, so he made them constantly jump through hoops to live up to his always over-the-top expectations.

Ron placed a sign-in sheet at *Vogue's* reception desk every morning, and the entire advertising staff was required to sign their names on it in the order of their arrival. Staffers arrived at the crack of dawn, hoping to be the first (second, third, or fourth) to sign "the sheet", and everyone who arrived after these early birds could see exactly who had already beaten them into the office that morning. At exactly 9:00am every day, this sheet was collected from our receptionist Silvia and reviewed by Ron. The only person who beat everyone into the office every morning was Ron himself.

Signing in at say 6:30-7:00am meant that you had a shot at having your name in one of the top spots on "the sheet". So an 8:30-8:45am arrival placed one squarely in the category of straggler. An 8:58am arrival time was duly noted, and required penance in the form of a crack of dawn entrance the next day. An entire week's worth of straggler arrivals required making it to one of the top spots on the sheet every day the following week. Claiming a top spot inspired silent envy among one's co-workers for the day, and the rare good word from Ron.

Ron was also famous for his 8:59am "bed checks". He would walk the 12th floor halls and peer into each individual office to confirm that his team, in its entirety, was present and accounted-for. If one had an early client meeting outside the office, it was necessary to alert Ron's assistant the night before, since missing a morning bed check was classified as a fire-able offense.

The Lesson: Since you too will need to adjust to your boss's unique quirks, figure out what they are ASAP. Arriving extremely early was Ron's thing, so success at *Vogue* demanded following suit.

#12: PINPOINT THE POWER PLAYERS

While Anna Wintour held the entire world at her feet--- which was *such* a source of pride inside *Vogue*--- it was Ron who made sure his power was acknowledged by everyone on the inside.

Reports spread of Ron wandering the editorial floor, doing "desk checks". Editorial assistants traded tales of returning to their seats to find this balding brawler waiting for them, no less demanding an explanation of their previous whereabouts. Just as said staffer was hopefully considering a call to Security, Ron would apparently scream at them, "Don't you know who the f—k I am???" This brash man must have no doubt appeared an oddity in this most rarified of settings--- *Vogue's* editorial offices on Condé Nast's 13th floor. But it took just one brush with Ron for anyone at *Vogue* to understand that he was a major player.

> **The Lesson: The people who run the place, beyond your own boss, need to be identified by little old you, oh say, immediately. Figure out Who is Who, and take note of how each interacts with the other within the organization. And acknowledge these people as players when you are in their presence.**

#13: MAKE SENSE OF THE SILLY STORIES

Still on the subject of Ron…

Ron often delivered colorful analogies to make a point. In one of our regular Monday afternoon meetings, we were in the throes of selling the September issue of *Vogue*. Ron, as usual, was obsessed with blowing the competition out of the water, *Harper's Bazaar* and *Elle* in particular, and decided to give us one of his many motivational speeches. Since it was early summer, Ron had weekends in the Hamptons on the brain, so he decided to draw a parallel between the different highways that one could possibly take to get to the Hamptons to the weighty-ness of September *Vogue*.

Ron likened the design houses, beauty companies, big retailers, and all other advertisers to people getting in their cars to best find their way to the Hamptons. Arriving in the Hamptons was supposed to embody "success" for us in this allegorical tale.

He told us, "You can take the Cross Island Parkway" (*Elle*), you can take the Northern State (*Harper's Bazaar*), or you can take the Long Island Expressway (*Vogue*). It's an obvious choice guys. The L.I.E. has the most lanes, gets you there the fastest, and everyone gets to see who else is driving on it. *And everybody who's anybody knows ya gotta take the F-----G L.I.E.*

to get to the Hamptons". The message? Go out and tell your clients not to advertise in *Harper's Bazaar* or *Elle*, and instead make them put every penny of their ad budgets into the September issue of *Vogue*. Our mission was to make the world-at-large see advertising in *Vogue* as the super highway to success.

> **The Lesson: People are often not straightforward when telling underlings what to do. In the situation above, I sat there in the *Vogue* Room wondering why Ron kept talking on and on about highways and the Hamptons. After all, didn't we work for a fashion magazine? I had to replay Ron's words in my head multiple times to understand what exactly we were supposed to do. Yet having finally made sense of his message, his dictate ironically still remains crystal clear to me, even all these years later. If your boss's directives sometimes don't make sense, do your best to decode them.**

#14: PREPARE FOR PERFECTION

During our weekly Monday meetings in the *Vogue* Room, "KISS"--- Keep It Simple Stupid--- was an expression we heard a lot, since it was Ron's favorite. Streamlining everything was ingrained into *Vogue's* culture, since there was never a minute to waste. From the pared down visual aesthetic of its offices, to the look of the people who inhabited them, there was an awe-inspiring sharp edge to everything inside *Vogue.*

Accomplishing everything at top speed required hard work on the front end to put operational efficiencies in place, which was worth all of the effort since the organization's workflow then ran through them. Priority one was getting it done.

At *Vogue*, KISS also applied to the importance of making everything look effortless. If, for example, one had had a harrowing commute to work, experienced an all-nighter with a sick child, or had any other unfortunate tale to tell, it was necessary to leave it behind. The strategy was to instead imply that one had simply sailed into work that day without incident. No one needed to know the dirty details, and no one wanted to hear excuses. Never complain, and never explain.

At *Vogue*, I learned that the key to making it look easy was an astonishing amount of advance planning. Said planning included making every consideration for what could possibly go wrong, and then putting advance "fixes" in place to avoid any slip-up that might possibly ensue. There were endless memos outlining every detail of every project, timelines put in place for every production, and written checklists for every execution.

There was a lot of synching of schedules, to include the coordination of each individual's arrival time and entrance at any *Vogue* event. Everything was pre-planned to the absolute enth, and then rolled out to make it look like we literally just thought of it.

The Lesson: Making it all look easy is an important skill to master. Finding oneself mired in avoidable surprises was unacceptable at *Vogue*, and it is not the way successful people go through life. *Vogue* streamlined its internal operating systems to make everything appear effortless, but the reality is we worked our fingers to the bone behind the scenes to give the impression of the exact opposite.

#15: THINK THIRTY STEPS AHEAD

Rather than planning for tomorrow, at *Vogue* one planned for the day after that, since tomorrow had of course been put to bed the day before. One spent this week planning for the ones two and three out, and this month working three to six ahead.

There were weekly status meetings during which we discussed every upcoming project in the pipeline to ensure everything was up to *Vogue's* exacting standards, and was moving forward with maximum speed and efficiency.

There were advance shipments made to off-site meetings or events--- always with cushion built in so that they arrived a day or two early--- if the shipment was lost, then there was still time to send yet another one. In this same spirit, it meant flying in the day before any important meeting with airline delays or cancellations in mind, never checking luggage onto an airplane and instead always carrying on, and traveling with as little as possible to include one's own wardrobe, since whatever one needed was sent ahead and confirmed as already there and waiting. No expense was spared in the name of getting it done before it needed to be.

This intense advance work allowed us to seemingly saunter into any meeting physically unencumbered, focused, and ready to wow "them"--- the design house, retailer, advertiser, or reader--- with our charms. The irony is that our blood, sweat and tears went into making it look like there was nothing to it.

> **The Lesson: When you are new to any job, always err on the side of over-anticipating and over-preparing for disaster--- as opposed to the opposite. This advance planning will require long hours and a lot of hard work, but your future success will depend on it.**

#16: *VOGUE'S* VOICE COACH: MR. HOW-NOW-BROWN-COW
Vogue's voice coach was an older British actor who worked out of his apartment in lower Manhattan. His home was filled to the brim with art, antiques, shabby chic sofas and lots and lots of books. During the colder months he and I often sat and enjoyed afternoon tea by the fire, before getting down to the work of improving me, which would take up the rest of our one-hour together.

In retrospect, I think this special "tea time" was my instructor's attempt to unwind my emotional state of mind. By our late afternoon visits I had already spent hours surviving inside *Vogue*, and it was difficult for me to transition from battle-ready to ready-for-my-cue. My instructor believed the key to speaking well in any setting is to be relaxed, and I always arrived for these appointments feeling anything but.

Those of us hired to speak to the press on *Vogue's* behalf were sent to work with its voice coach. Also selected were staffers in whom *Vogue* detected any unpleasant accent, no matter how slight. Outside of *Vogue*, his other clients included an impressive collection of corporate figureheads, to include at the time the CEO of IBM, who depended on him to help prep for big speeches or upcoming press conferences.

This man had his subjects repeat, "how now brown cow" over and over again as a warm-up exercise at the beginning of every session. He showed us how to pronounce it in an exaggerated fashion, enunciating every syllable in such an over the top fashion that it resulted in mouth contortions. The man swore that mastering the proper elocution of this particular phrase was, for whatever reason, key. Back at *Vogue* we referred to him as Mr. How-Now-Brown-Cow, and only those of us who worked with him were in on the joke.

Having spent most of his career on the London stage, he felt strongly that one could only speak well if one's lungs were properly filled with air. So we practiced breathing in and out, a lot. We practiced when to breathe, which was during the few seconds before we spoke. We practiced when to let the air out, which was gradually and as we spoke. He tried to impart to his voice students a physicality of which actors are keenly aware, but the rest of us are most likely not.

He also believed in filming his subjects as they spoke, and there was a lot of post-game analysis. He pointed out any fidgeting, shifting, movement or anything else on camera that might visually distract the person to whom one was speaking. Mr. How-Now-Brown-Cow saw self-conscious gestures as an assault to this concept of seamlessness whether one was talking to a single person or to a group. In other words, if people are busy watching you shift side-to-side in your seat as you speak to them, they are less likely to remember afterward what you actually said.

There was also a lot of visualization in the mind's eye and focus on the power of positive thinking--- since success is a self-fulfilling concept. His strategy was to unleash in his students the power to command any encounter by channeling the excitement and brimming enthusiasm to see them that the people on the other end actually *felt*.

As I wrestled to find my *Vogue* footing against the backdrop of this marquee concept, Mr. How-Now-Brown-Cow assured me that the CEO of IBM struggled too.

Lesson One: Everyone is a work in progress with regard to the ability to verbally communicate to the world at large. Apparently, at the time, even the CEO of IBM. Work hard on being able to sound your best

in conversation with anyone and everyone, and work on editing out any distracting habits because the reality is that most of us have at least a few.

Lesson Two: Even though you are not yet the CEO of IBM, or from someplace as glamorous as *Vogue*---people are still likely excited to hear what you have to say. So relax enough to be yourself when speaking with people you have just met. Work to channel the enthusiasm and excitement of being there that Mr. How-Now-Brown-Cow felt so strongly about.

#17: GOD PROTECTS SMALL CHILDREN, DRUNKS, & THOSE WHO STAY ON MESSAGE FOR *VOGUE*

Every month, I met with *Vogue's* readers, advertisers, ad agencies, and trade groups in New York and cities all across the country. My job title was Merchandising Editor, and as such my mission was to message on the magazine's behalf, put a face on *Vogue,* and bring the editorial content for that particular season to life for all of these important people. There to document everything were TV crews, print reporters, photographers, and the P.R. people who had secured previous permission from the magazine to interview me.

What exactly does message on the magazine's behalf mean?

At the end of each season's fashion runway shows, Anna would summon the advertising team into the *Vogue* Room to outline for us "the stories for the season". To hear *Anna Wintour* outline the background color for a particular story from start-to-finish provided an incredible glimpse into the planning process of an iconic editor, and of the living legend variety no less.

Anna crystalized for us in this meeting the colors, fabrics, silhouettes and other key concepts that *Vogue* would "stand behind" on its pages in the coming months. And that which Anna communicated to us was in turn to be immediately disseminated by us to our readers, advertisers, and everyone else. This dissemination is what I mean by messaging. And getting the messaging exactly right mattered, a lot, to *Vogue*.

Anna had her own in-house P.R. Director, who tracked everything said to the press on the magazine's behalf. Like clock work, this P.R. Director would show up in my office doorway to announce, "another good month!" She would then drop onto my desk a pile of press clippings, video, etc. containing quotes from me. "Another good month" meant I got to keep my job.

When I was hired by *Vogue*, I had absolutely no background in speaking with the press. So I was trained on the job by the magazine to speak to the other media on its behalf. It took me about a year to finally be able to walk into a room of waiting press with anything close to the poise and visible polish that *Vogue* expected of me. Worse, learning on the job for me meant having my every public move sent back to *Vogue* and reviewed by *Anna Wintour's office*.

I felt ill, often, just thinking about it.

But I did pull it off. I did it one event at a time. And before I knew it I could look back and point to a track record of satisfactory work. The secret of my success was to work within the outline of Anna's seasonal dictates when answering any question asked of me, and to remember that when I was speaking with any member of the press--- or to an advertiser or reader--- the magazine and I were, at that moment, one and the same.

> **Lesson One: Make sure that any message you deliver to the outside world on your company's behalf will stand up to internal scrutiny, and to do this have a seasonal script. Every organization has its own script--- even if they do not have Anna Wintour at the helm to conceptualize it and formally outline it for everyone.**
>
> **Figure out what the messaging should be for your company, and create a script in your head so you can speak to the outside world on your organization's behalf, even if it is in an informal fashion. And tailor within this larger script, in each specific situation,**

according to your individual audience. This big picture concept is that much more important today on social media, where we witness fast and loose oversharing with such disturbing frequency. Also important is to revisit said script every few months to avoid sounding stale, and to make sure that you are operating with your company's most updated information.

Lesson Two: To have Anna Wintour looking over my shoulder as I communicated to the outside world, in what I would argue was my first real job, felt like starring--- daily --- in my own worst nightmare come to life. Looking back I really can't believe I survived this trying time, but I did.

#18: SHIPWRECKED WITH SEBASTIAN JUNGER

What one person perceives to be disaster, another might see as success. Everyone who knows me knows that I never advocate cover-ups, but if events before your eyes unfold negatively do not sound the alarm right away. Instead proceed at full steam, take stock of how others see the situation, and tweak all next steps accordingly.

One day, my phone rang and it was our Condé Nast Corporate Office asking me to attend an event they were planning. The event would take place at Macy's Herald Square, and spotlight a reading by Sebastian Junger to promote his newly released book *"The Perfect Storm"*. Would I mind simply showing up, they asked, so they could put *Vogue's* name on the event invitation, the event in-store signage, and the press release they planned to send out? When Condé Nast Corporate called, one never said "no". So my answer to their request, without hesitation, was "yes".

The night of the event arrived, and the outline of the program seemed straightforward enough. Sebastian would sit on a stool with a microphone in a highly trafficked area of the store, and read from his book. Next to Sebastian, Condé Nast would set up signage with his headshot and the cover image of his book--- so that Macy's shoppers would know that it was indeed *the* Sebastian Junger in our presence, reading his own work.

My Condé Nast Corporate contact explained to me that crowds of Macy's shoppers would simply stop and gather to listen to Sebastian, after he was introduced by me, and began to read his own work.

We set up for the event about an hour before the start time, and at 6:15 Sebastian sauntered in looking every inch like, well, Sebastian Junger---very rugged and ready for adventure. He arrived holding a copy of his book. On our end we had the microphone, stool and sign. So it looked like we were all set.

For whatever reason, Macy's P.R. Office did not send someone to assist us during the event, which would have been corporate protocol. So it was just my Condé Nast Corporate contact, and me. And Sebastian. The program outline was so simple, in fact, that my Corporate contact asked me if she could leave at the start of the program to go home to her kids in Carnegie Hill. Since no one said no to Condé Nast Corporate, "of course!" was my response.

At exactly 6:30pm Sebastian started reading. Not one person stopped to listen. Sebastian kept reading. No one noticed. Throngs of Macy's shoppers barreled through our event area, each with their sights set on some triple-marked-down-deal they had just heard about via some in-store announcement. And, for some reason, every item these people just-had-to-have sat somewhere behind Sebastian on his stool. The stampede of shoppers nearly knocked him off his seat a number of times.

I was prepared to problem solve. I stopped passers-by, offering to introduce them to Sebastian Junger, the one and only, should any of them agree to stick around until the end of his reading. Every shopper seemed to look straight through me, and kept moving. It was, unfortunately, not a literary crowd.

I feared that this favor for Corporate was the one to be my final undoing, and that my *Vogue* days were now quite likely over. After an eternity, Sebastian finished reading. I thanked him. Boldly, I told him how proud we were at *Vogue* and Condé Nast to have had him host the evening's event at Macy's. Sebastian appeared entirely unflustered. I never mentioned to him in our final exchange that this calamity was the worst I had ever witnessed.

Patrons at The Half King, the lower Manhattan pub that Sebastian opened in 2000, still show up in the evenings hoping to get a glimpse of him. The rest of the well-read Manhattan set trips over one another for access to him. Ironic, I know.

I was sure Sebastian Junger would leave Macy's and immediately call his publicist to describe that other perfect storm, the one that had been his evening with me. For anyone, it should have been the next step.

At 8:30 the next morning, my Condé Nast Corporate contact called my office to report that the event had been "a huge success". I mustered back in response that "it had indeed been just that". I wondered who her sources were, or if she had maybe just made some up. In that moment I breathed an enormous sigh of relief and privately thanked Sebastian Junger for either lying through his teeth, or for simply keeping his mouth shut. I still believe he did the latter.

There is so much to learn here, and we can break it into four parts.

Lesson One: Know your audience. Make sure any material you choose to present will be of interest not just to you, but also to those to whom you will present it. Condé Nast Corporate could have gone anywhere else to find a more appropriate audience for a literary lion. And since Condé Nast Corporate's marketing efforts were always completely crackerjack, I never thought to doubt them. This was a momentary blind spot for them, and for me. And in retrospect I cannot believe that Sebastian Junger ever agreed to do this event. Condé Nast Corporate could have picked any place besides Macy's Herald Square, home of the Door Busters promotion, if their objective was to showcase Sebastian's *"The Perfect Storm"*. Furthermore, Macy's shoppers were underserved since the evening's program was just so obviously not up their alley. Sebastian Junger at Macy's was a bad idea from the beginning.

Lesson Two: If things do not go well, at a party or during a presentation for example, do not immediately admit personal defeat. Instead, focus only on the positive that came out of the meeting, project, or partnership. Do not zero in on the mistakes you think you made in the process. From where you sit, the most important thing is to make "them"--- the client, your boss, or both--- see first and foremost any dividends reaped from your hard work.

Lesson Three: The next time you agree to do anyone a favor, think through the possible pitfalls ahead of time. Your goal is not to get left holding the proverbial bag. Learn to think seven steps ahead at all times, to anticipate any and every worst-case scenario that could transpire. Line up solutions ahead of time, in case the worst does happen to you, because at some point it will.

Lesson Four: Develop the ability to put everything in context, and don't forget to look back and laugh. The story above left me deeply scarred and for too long. But cast in a different light, and this time as a cautionary tale, it suddenly seems comical--- even to me.

#19: MANAGE THE STRESS

There was a tremendous amount of pressure at *Vogue*. It could be physically felt, and the stress levels often had people so on edge that many days had an-everyone-out-for-themself feel to them. One spring afternoon, it took its toll on one of the nicest people at *Vogue* (and a luminary no less), who left the building in an ambulance. Either the stress of intra-office politics had overcome him, or he had had a heart attack. Or both.

I am pleased to report that stress-of-office politics was indeed the diagnosis, and that this lovely man lived on to fight another day. While this particular story ends well, it registers an important point.

In every work setting, you will encounter people who feel it is their job to push your buttons and see what you are made of. Size up these situations and take charge of them, or they will end up owning you. Take a deep breath, and put an action plan in place to put your detractors back in that corner where they belong.

To pull this off, you will need "people".

Cultivate friendships in your work setting with people who you hopefully admire, or at least like well enough. One of these people should be at your level--- so you can confide in them and commiserate a bit. Another key confidante should be higher than you, so they can operate day-to-day within the organization in a got-your-back-fashion.

> **The Lesson: Know that in any new job, someone will be out to get you. Bad things happen to good people, and at some point they will happen to you. Use your pre-selected people to protect and politic for you inside the organization.**

#20: LIFE IS LIKE A FASHION SHOW

Let me begin by describing what goes on at a fashion show, and I will lead by telling you that every designer runway unveiling is pure theatre.

First, there is the matter of who is invited. Each designer's invitation list is a carefully curated collection of personalities. People make the cut, or they don't. When the invitations go out, some egos are boosted and some are quite bruised.

Then there is the pecking order of seating assignments, and here please picture an Eighth Grade popularity contest. Who you are is where you sit, and everyone in the room knows that one's placement signifies his or her professional importance, or pitiful lack thereof. The honor of having actually been invited to the show is now entirely negated if one is seated in a lesser spot.

Designers spend weeks working on the seating: they place front row adversaries on opposite sides of one another (*Vogue* and *Harper's Bazaar*), rival department stores far apart (Bergdorf Goodman and Barneys). The closer to the front row one is seated, the more relevant one is in the mix--- and the opposite is true too. The rest of the media fills in between factions, the important outlets sprinkled like fairy dust and made highly visible--- and the less prestigious publications relegated to the rafters.

Ironically, a remarkable number of individuals in the room see this as *their* moment to shine, more so than the designer's. The fashion show itself is just a setting, and an excuse, for these same individuals to re-direct the spotlight onto themselves.

There are many competing agendas in the mix, so by the time this cast of characters has assembled for the big event, everything has already been put in place. The department stores will have waged epic battles over the right to carry hand-picked exclusive pieces from the collection, and buyers from each store will have already written up their orders before the "unveiling". The media will have taken each other out behind the scenes to get their hands on their favorite looks, and they will have hijacked the samples and already shot them for publication (*Vogue* always wins the war). The Publicists will have collected the color and are ready to release seconds after the designer's bow. Finally, the celebrities in the audience will have been hand picked, and carefully placed, to make sure the whole room comes to a boil at just the right moment.

So while a fashion runway show might look like a debut, it is actually instead about showcasing a body of work which is mostly complete--- and everyone in the room is focused on promoting his or her role in the process. Anyone walking into a fashion show thinking it is an actual debut is operating in a vacuum.

Life is like a fashion show.

Prior to any professional gathering, invitees will discreetly check ahead with the organizers to see who else is invited to the event. They will then do due diligence to identify other attendees' individual agendas to compare them to their own for this upcoming meeting--- even if one's only agenda is simply to figure out someone else's. Individuals will then put plans in place to further--- or up-end--- any other attendee's agenda.

To accomplish this, factions will form in advance, and each will decide privately beforehand what it wants to say, and to whom, and when, and why. Each will stage mini-meetings, or if this is not possible will hold a conference call ahead of time, to outline next steps for constituents.

And when these pre-formed factions all arrive in the same room for the "big meeting", or professional social gathering, each will observe the others' placement in it, standing or seated. Individuals from each will position themselves near certain people and away from others, according to already outlined objectives.

The reality is that "a meeting" is usually not in any way the beginning of an idea--- it is often the physical embodiment of the end of a process. The meeting itself is often about putting finishing touches on that which is almost complete--- and the "publicists" are most likely ready to press send.

The Lesson: Before any meeting, or any work cocktail party/dinner, dig up what is *really* going on behind the scenes. This way, you will be properly informed before you walk into the room.

And upon arrival, observe people's placement in it. Make a mental note of who is sitting where and why. Equipped with this necessary color, you can decide whether to drop yourself into the mix, or stay out of the fray, depending on how you feel about what is about to happen.

And pay close attention if someone calls a "brainstorming meeting", since the chances are excellent that someone's goal is to get the group to "think" of an idea that is in reality already in development.

#21: TEN THINGS *VOGUE* STAFFERS KNEW TO GET THE JOB, THAT YOU SHOULD NOW KNOW TOO

UNDERSTAND THE IMPORTANCE OF THE THANK-YOU NOTE

If you meet (or speak) with anyone, formally or informally, as part of your professional journey, write the person a thank-you note. If any individual takes the time to offer you advice of any kind, or does a favor for you (big or small), follow up with a thank-you note. Do not underestimate the power of expressing appreciation to someone who has helped you in some way. Your goal is to cut through the corporate clutter and stand out against a backdrop of hundreds or even thousands of other job candidates. For this purpose (and many others) the thank-you note is your way of getting noticed.

You will need to do the following in this note: 1) register that it was thoughtful of the person to meet with you, and for them to have also shared thoughts on their experience working at the company 2) reference two or three things that the two of you discussed during your time together, and also highlight what you learned about both the company *and* the person you met 3) include one or two sentences telling them, not why you are so great but instead, what you will *do* for this company for which you would like to work.

No candidate was offered a job at *Vogue* until a thank-you note was received by every individual who had interviewed the prospective new-hire. Nothing could, or would, proceed with a job offer at *Vogue* until all of these notes were received. It was extremely common to hear discussion in *Vogue's* hallways that someone had "received the note" and that they were calling HR to let them know the job could be offered to the candidate.

In this electronic era, it is increasingly acceptable to send this thank-you note by email. But optimal follow-up requires mailing a second note in hardcopy fashion, *in addition* to the email. If you are applying to work in a bank or other very-suited corporate setting, this hardcopy follow-up should be typewritten. In other industries like fashion, media, or perhaps technology (of the smaller start-up variety), or when thanking someone for what is purely an informational interview (where there is no actual job available), a hand written note is better.

> **The Lesson: Write a note to absolutely everyone you meet with during any interview process, and double check of course that you have spelled the recipient's first and last names correctly. If possible, you should also include the person's business title when addressing the envelope, and double check to make sure that you have his or her title written correctly. When in doubt, just go with the correctly spelled first and last name, and omit the person's business title.**

IF YOU'RE ON TIME, YOU'RE LATE

To be successful at *Vogue*, punctuality was paramount. It made a point, one as sharp as the heels we wore walking *Vogue's* halls.

> **The Lesson: Always arrive 5-10 minutes early for any job interview, or important meeting of any kind.**

BODY LANGUAGE

First impressions count for everything, and self-presentation is key. You will need to do the following when greeting anyone for any reason in a work setting: stand up straight, look them directly in the eye, and offer an especially firm handshake. At *Vogue*, we looked for these qualities first and foremost in any job candidate.

> **The Lesson: In reality you have about two minutes to sell yourself during this initial encounter, as the interviewer will make quick observations about you during this time frame. The steps outlined above are the key to making a good impression in any job interview (or social gathering), if you want to get the encounter off to a good start.**

SPEAK WELL

Everyone is a work in progress with regard to his or her ability to verbally communicate to the world at large. Work hard on your ability to sound your best in conversation with anyone and everyone.

> **The Lesson: Walk into any job interview having developed the ability to tell someone what you think about any particular subject, and why. What counts most is to have an informed opinion on the given subject--- from current events in the news to day-to-day developments in any given industry.**

WRITE WELL

One did a lot of writing at *Vogue*: marketing proposals for advertisers, partnership proposals to high level charities, larger press communications, internal and external memos, and client thank you notes. It was very valuable at *Vogue* to be able to write extremely well, and in an authentic and personal style.

During my first days on the job, these projects took me too long by internal standards. While my academic writing style had to date served me well--- I quickly realized it needed to "translate" into the real world. At *Vogue*, I learned to make my point quickly, and to condense my thoughts into a less-is-much-more writing style.

I also found it extremely helpful to adopt *Vogue's* very own alliterative style of writing. Below, please find an example from the November 2012 issue (copied verbatim, to include the all-caps placements):

VOGUE
point of view
PARTY PEOPLE

Some women blow up a gale wherever they go. They just can't help it. Rihanna is one; so is Kate Upton. They're very different stars, but Rihanna and Kate share this INBORN ABILITY to---- just by stepping through a door--- draw a chattering crowd that whirls like CHARGED ELECTRONS around a nucleus. Wherever they are, the party is.

Imagine having that kind of CHARISMA. On some levels, that's what fashion is all about: creating an affirming hum around yourself by your choice of adornment and array.

The CELEBRATORY SEASON is approaching, and so we're RSVPing by throwing a few attention-getting CURVEBALLS. There's a new slouchy, lounge-y after-dark chic in town that--- while unpretentious and easy to wear--- has an ineffable air of ELEGANT DARING. It delivers an easy-on, easy-off languor that's hard to ignore.

You might not be a bikini model with 536,125 followers on Twitter. You might not be a chart-topping GLAMOUR GODDESS with a bevy of Grammys under your belt. But you can certainly CAPTIVATE A ROOM with a few strokes and seams of originality.

The Lesson: To learn to write well in the real world---
just like in the college world--- one must practice,
practice, practice. At *Vogue* I adapted my writing
style to a more condensed and obviously alliterative
one, since it allows me to make my point faster and
with the appearance of ease. Effective written com-
munication is increasingly critical in today's 24/7 on-
line world, which demands clever rapid response of
everyone in it to include you.

NO OBVIOUSLY DISTRACTING HABITS

Everyone has them, so to determine what they are is key. Even more important is to make sure that you find a way to make them go away. Fidgeting, nail
biting, whatever--- it is important to determine whatever the issue might be to
get control of it.

The Lesson: Have someone stage a mock interview
starring you, and film it so you can visualize, scruti-
nize and edit out those habits. And never chew gum
in public. Never have anything in your mouth when
speaking with anyone else--- cough drops, breath
mints, or candy for example. And make sure that
there are never any sounds in the form of a nervous
habit or for whatever reason.

SPEAK THE LANGUAGE OF THE INDUSTRY

Every industry speaks its own language. It is critical that you identify the lexi-
con of the industry in which you wish to work and then learn to speak it too.

The Lesson: As with the study of any foreign language, immersion delivers the best results. Read your
industry's trade publications, and listen to interviews
given by those doing what you wish to do. Mimic

their vocabulary, and copy their slang, to project an
air of belonging.

VISIBLE POLISH

Polish is adopting an air of ease in any new situation. It is having one's thoughts collected enough to be present in the moment and give the appearance of being calmly in control. It is the also hard earned confidence that empowers you to showcase your very best self to others. Polish is not just admirable--- it is the critical component for accomplishment in today's often crushingly competitive business world.

Once associated with a privileged background, polish is instead developed through education. Visible polish arrives through a level of self-awareness with regard to one's own strengths and weaknesses--- both the commitment to smooth out the latter, and spotlight the former. Eventually, it becomes habit.

> **The Lesson: Polish is *the* secret weapon that allows**
> **you to immediately and authentically connect with**
> **strangers, and make them quickly like and respect**
> **you. Visible polish inspires these same strangers to**
> **align with you to get things done.**

ALWAYS WEAR A SUIT TO AN INTERVIEW

If called to interview for a job at *Vogue*, protocol dictated that one wore a suit. One that was well cut, neutral in color (black, navy, charcoal) and form flattering--- not too tight yet never boxy. This same suit should be accented with smart accessories--- good shoes with some heel on them, a simple handbag (go with understated and no bling), and spare jewelry that does not distract.

> **The Lesson: If you are interviewing for a job in a**
> **creative industry such as fashion, advertising, or me-**
> **dia--- wear a suit. The same holds true when inter-**
> **viewing for a job in finance, law, or politics, and in the**

non-profit world. Unless you are interviewing to be a fashion stylist, wear a suit.

IMAGINE IN YOUR MIND THE ULTIMATE OUTCOME, AND HOPEFULLY IT WILL HAPPEN

If you think positively, positive things will happen. Not always, but often. The inverse is usually true, in that if you worry about the worst unfolding you actually increase the chances of making it happen.

When interviewing at *Vogue* it helped to appear like you had already been there, even if secretly most of us knew we had far from arrived.

> **The Lesson: The ability to exude confidence is an important quality to develop. So add "put-on-game-face" to your morning "To Do" list, since success is a self-fulfilling concept.**

RUN EVERYTHING PAST EVERYONE INVOLVED
God help any staffer who allowed *Vogue's* name to appear on any invitation, piece of signage, advertisement, or in any other promotional capacity without first running it up the flagpole within *Vogue's* walls. No use of the *Vogue* name and logo was too small for securing permission within the organization.

> **The Lesson: Before you release for public viewing anything with your organization's name on it--- or anyone else's name on it for that matter--- secure advanced approval from *all* parties involved. Period.**

GOSSIP GIRL
Pay attention to gossip, since where there is smoke, there is fire. The key to survival at *Vogue* was to traffic in information to avoid surprises. Embrace this critical workplace concept, and you will be successful. Buck this important tenet, and you will suffer.

At *Vogue,* any time we heard whispers of someone in the building "going to Heaven" we knew it spelled trouble. "Heaven" was a particular department in our Condé Nast Corporate office, where they sent people with big titles at magazines to work "in a different capacity" for the company. Everyone knew that anyone sent to Heaven would be shown the door within months.

So any talk of Heaven was big news. And if it was your boss who was the subject of these discussions and therefore likely leaving imminently, then either 1) you were getting a new boss soon or 2) you were possibly getting fired too--- without, of course, the courtesy of being sent to Heaven first.

Any chatter on the subject of Heaven required appropriate next steps, to prepare for whatever lay ahead.

> **The Lesson: Pay close attention to the chit-chat going on around you, get involved, ask follow-up questions, and collect information as you go along in your daily routine.**

NEVER HOLD A MEETING THAT LASTS MORE THAN ONE HOUR

A half hour to forty-five minutes will also often suffice. Never fill time in a meeting just because someone has allotted it to you.

> **The Lesson: Get to the point as quickly as possible, and don't grandstand. Keep it simple stupid, and declare the meeting over at the earliest possible moment.**

BE FUTURE FOCUSED

Work hard to develop the ability to intuit what will happen--- before it happens. Pay close attention to what is going on, both before your eyes and behind the scenes, and rely on your instincts to predict any outcome. Once in place, your unique spider-sense will serve you well.

> **The Lesson: The ability to see the future before it happens is an asset inside any organization, and it will save you the wasted effort of cleaning up major messes after they occur. More importantly, the ability to see things before they happen will make you a standout in any industry.**

THERE WILL BE DRUDGERY

Most of it will be obvious to you: it will entail fetching coffee, picking up lunches, lifting boxes, shipping packages, cleaning closets, and running random errands. In a separate category will fall requests that appear to make no sense, and will instead seem to waste your precious time.

One day, for example, I remember thinking to myself (but would never have actually uttered out loud at *Vogue*): "Really, you want me to fly out to Los Angeles this weekend to make sure Amber Valetta walks down a runway at an advertiser event in the correct dress? Seriously? This will be my ninth weekend in a row to travel for work. Can't *anyone*, in oh say LA, handle this one?"

Needless to say, I got on a plane without complaint that Friday morning, and returned home late that Sunday night.

In between, I had fun hanging out with Amber, who, it turns out, has a great sense of humor. And a million people would have loved to trade places with me.

> **The Lesson: Drudgery, real or perceived, will annoy you. But chances are it's not that bad. Just say yes, and put the task behind you as quickly as possible.**

UNDERPROMISE AND OVER-DELIVER

When assigned a particular project, give the person who assigned it to you a completion date that you know you can more than meet. This way, you will have given yourself cushion, should you for any reason need more time to get it done.

And promise to do that which has been assigned with a smile on your face and a sense of enthusiasm. Then do your best to deliver work (on time or early) that exceeds their expectations, catches them off guard in a good way, and allows them--- your boss, co-worker, or client--- to get a glimpse into that of which you are actually capable.

> **The Lesson: When committing to a deadline, allow yourself enough of a window to complete the assignment on time, if not before the due date. Promise to execute a task that is up to the job, but deliver something that instead reveals your inner star quality.**

THE CLIENT ALWAYS COMES FIRST

Every successful organization thinks outside itself, and puts the client first. At *Vogue*, this meant channeling the desires of its readers and advertisers first and foremost, and navigating accordingly to serve them.

> **The Lesson: Some individuals inside the organization lost sight of this tenet on occasion, choosing to**

instead prioritize their own advancement over that of the organization. But two people who never forgot this important principle were Ron and Anna.

AVOID CONFLICTS OF INTEREST AT ALL COSTS

Always be on the lookout for any conflict of interest in the mix. It might seem tempting in the moment to prioritize personal gains over long-term organizational interests, but you risk sinking the ship by thinking short-term. *Vogue* absolutely always took the institutional long view, and you should too.

> **The Lesson: Study the years leading up to the 2008 financial crash, when a faction in finance schemed to inflate their annual Christmas bonuses through a series of intentional misrepresentations. Their actions sparked a crisis in banking and far beyond, and eventually brought the entire U.S. economy to a standstill.**
>
> **Okay this is an epic example, but it makes an important point. Always put the integrity of the organization first, since short-term thinking can have a cascading and catastrophic effect.**
>
> **And distance yourself from individuals who put personal agendas above the best interests of the organization for whom you both work. These people ultimately tend to get spit out of the mix, either before or *after* they do the place real damage. Make it your priority not to be associated with their self-serving ways.**

FORGIVE BUT DO NOT FORGET

If someone does something to you behind your back, works overtly (or covertly) against you, or takes action to weaken your professional position--- or personal reputation--- take note and file it away in your head.

And never forget it. Vow instead to distance yourself from them in an imperceptible yet firm fashion.

> **The Lesson: If they did it once, they will do it again. You have just caught a glimpse into the true character of this individual, so make sure you never again let this person catch you with your guard down.**

PERCEPTION IS REALITY

The outside world perceives reality as it sees it at any given moment.

If the world thinks you have a problem, then you do--- and you must appear to take steps to fix it.

The inverse is, of course, also true. For example, at the time I never shared the Sebastian Junger story with anyone inside *Vogue*. So when Condé Nast Corporate called to congratulate me on my success the morning after the debacle, my perfect storm of a problem evaporated in an instant.

And Corporate then called the top brass at *Vogue* to tell them what a fabulous job I did for them the night before.

So what did I do? I kept my mouth shut.

> **The Lesson: Look outside yourself to assess how the world sees any particular situation--- and tailor all next steps accordingly. If your boss or your client's perception is that there is a problem, then it is necessary to take next steps to solve the situation, even if it feels like going through the motions for the sake of public appearances.**
>
> **And only very rarely will you instead catch a break, like I did with Sebastian.**

PEOPLE WANT TO WORK WITH PEOPLE THEY LIKE

And they want to work with people who they trust.

> **The Lesson: One's personal reputation counts for everything in any industry. Be careful before you pull**

any punches in any work setting, especially when you are young and unknown. For your boss and your co-workers to like you, and trust you, counts for a lot.

IF YOU SEE BAD THINGS COMING, GET OUT WHILE YOU CAN

During my last six months at *Vogue*, there were Condé Nast rumors galore on the subject of Richard ("Mad Dog") Beckman's impending arrival as *Vogue's* new Publisher. The feeling inside the building was that as much as Ron was at the top of his game and had maximized *Vogue* as serious cash cow (to put it mildly), his days at the magazine were, for whatever reason, numbered. I could handle Ron since I genuinely liked and respected him, and most importantly had been hired by him. But since the Publisher dictates the culture inside any media entity, and usually wants to bring in his or her own people, "Mad Dog" was someone who I felt desperate to avoid at all costs.

About a month after I left *Vogue*, Richard Beckman arrived as Publisher. Famous for hanging a bell outside his office and for ringing it every time a new advertising page was sold, Mad Dog was a bull in a china shop and made Ron Galotti look, well, far more desirable as an alternative. Richard Beckman quickly became notorious for a particular event that transpired a couple of months into his stay, during *Vogue's* annual sales meeting, a three-day event that Anna never missed. Declaring to two female staffers in his distinctive British accent--- and in an extremely drunken state according to my eyewitnesses in the room--- "I want to see you two kiss", Mad Dog smashed together the heads of two higher-up *Vogue* female staffers.

During said smashing, Mad Dog broke the nose of one of these women. The victim worked in our LA office, was in town for the sales meeting, and was a big boa wearer. *Vogue* was back in the headlines in *The New York Post* and other New York tabloids for at least a week as they reported the salacious details of the encounter. The LA boa wearer was reported to have sued Condé Nast for $1 million in damages, and won.

The Lesson: Ron was crazy like a fox, but more than merited the title of *Vogue* media mogul in the opinion of all who worked for him. Mad Dog's staffers worried he had rabies. Those who left ahead of Richard's arrival did so with their careers intact and their heads together. Those who departed during Richard's reign of terror left in a shattered emotional state. Sometimes it's hard to admit, but the arrival of new management is always followed by changes to the company culture. Don't let yourself be caught flat-footed. Instead, always be ready to take it on the road if need be.

#23 FIFTEEN LIFE LESSONS LEARNED AT *VOGUE* WHICH APPLY TO ANY WORK SETTING

EVERYTHING IN LIFE IS A BUSINESS
Vogue is first and foremost a business. At the end of the day, all of our efforts were for naught if we were unable to *sell* the magazine--- to readers and advertisers--- to fund the editorial budgets, pay the staff and keep the magazine in the black so we could do it all over again the next month.

> **The Lesson: Whatever organization you work for, never forget that at the end of the day everything is a business--- non-profits, schools, churches, etc. It all boils down to dollars and cents to keep any operation afloat.**

ASSOCIATE YOURSELF WITH BIG BRANDS EARLY IN YOUR CAREER
My own resume lists Bergdorf Goodman, *Vogue*, and *The New York Times* (a total of 14 years at these three companies combined). The associated credibility of these three brands still serves me well.

The Lesson: Try to collect well-known names on your resume at the beginning of your career. The credibility of their association from once upon a time will never leave you.

THE FIRST YEAR OF ANY NEW JOB--- OR ANY NEW VENTURE---- IS THE HARDEST

At *Vogue*, after the first day, or perhaps the first week, the reality of the job set in. By the three-month mark, the glow was gone. Instead the stress and raw expectations of the day-to-day demands felt overwhelming, and my entire existence felt very shaky. Everyday, I was convinced that I could be fired. At the six-month mark, I felt like I was on firmer ground, and by then thank God had some success to point to. By the nine-month mark, a sigh of relief came over me, since it felt like I was nearing a threshold. At the one-year anniversary of my arrival at *Vogue*, I was privately pleased to look back on a productive year--- and to have the transition behind me.

The Lesson: Every additional three months in *any* new job--- or any new adventure--- marks an important milestone during the first year. Take it one day at a time, and you too will come out on the other end intact and better for the experience.

SOME DAYS YOU'RE HOT, SOME DAYS YOU'RE NOT

Some days it will feel like you are on a tear. You somehow caught a wave and are magnificently riding it to shore. Your future looks bright.

Other days you will walk into the office and not know what hit you. External forces will feel inexplicably aligned against you. It is as if you are a star in the night sky: bright and shiny one minute, falling the next.

The Lesson: You will have good days and bad days. Hear me now. You will have some very bad days in the work world, and no one escapes this reality. If you are able to remember that you are not immune to this

universal truth, it will help you maintain important perspective when the world seems out to get you.

POSITION THINGS POSITIVELY

It is not what you say; it is how you say it. People usually respond first and foremost to how things are being said, and then process the content. You can minimize fallout in difficult situations by choosing your words, and your tone, very carefully.

> **The Lesson: The importance of positioning things positively applies to any job or real life situation. And as a parent, I think this is invaluable advice.**

EVERYONE ON A FIRST NAME BASIS

Use everyone's first name, from the security guard, to the messenger, to the front desk receptionist. Take the time to learn the first names of those whose important work might not be noticeable to others far less astute than you. Do this not just for the right reasons (which are too numerous to count) but also because these same people can and will help you in ways that you will surely underestimate when you start any new job. You will quickly wonder how you might have otherwise survived without these new allies.

> **The Lesson: Introduce yourself to the people who you will see day to day in any work setting, learn their first names, and use them.**

SEND OUT SMOKE SIGNALS

Professional or personal, small or big--- do not try to go it alone. Small problems can quickly become big headaches if not immediately nipped in the bud.

> **The Lesson: Find a trusted friend or mentor and confidentially ask them for guidance absolutely**

immediately before you do any particular situation, and yourself, real damage.

CUT THROUGH THE NOISE AND STAY FOCUSED

In life, and in any work setting, you will receive disproportionately more criticism than praise, in spite of your really good work and measurable success. People don't often go out of their way to compliment someone who deserves it, since they have most likely moved on to the next project in their heads and forgot to give credit for a job well done in the immediate past. Sadly, you are more likely to only hear from people when they feel something needs fixing, or when they are convinced that for some reason the situation requires their critical input. Learn to distinguish between valuable feedback, and plain old negative noise.

> **The Lesson: If anyone takes the time to say something nice about your work--- or anything complimentary about your personal qualities--- definitely take it to heart. And *do* replay these same words over and over in your head the next time you need a lift.**

WHAT COMES AROUND GOES AROUND

Treat everyone else as you would want to be treated. Those who put positive energy into the universe tend to have good things come back to them. People who spew out negative actions into the larger sphere often get them back in spades.

> **The Lesson: Justice rides a slow horse, but eventually it does deliver.**

MEET & GREET, GRIP & GRIN

At *Vogue*, my favorite category of event to attend was one we called a "meet & greet, grip & grin". All of the other events I attended required that I not only advance plan every detail for them (in cities across the country), but also formally host them as the face of *Vogue* to audiences of readers, advertisers, trade groups, etc. On top of that, it was expected that I grant interviews on-site to members of the TV and print press who were on hand to ask "*Vogue*" questions of me ("What does *Vogue* think about the color green for spring?"). In these situations, I had a limitless list of things to attend to.

Which is why I loved a good old "meet & greet, grip & grin". All I had to do was show up at the event, walk around a room of perfect strangers, and introduce myself to the hosts, event VIPS, and anyone else who seemed up for a chat. I was flown to cities like LA and Miami for these events and was incredulous that *Vogue* paid for these trips, since to me they seemed like boondoggles and my responsibilities were minimal. And yet, the most remarkable connections were made during these encounters. They reaped very real professional dividends for me, and separately for *Vogue* of course.

> **The Lesson: Attend any event that you are invited to, and see it as an opportunity. Show up. Mix, mingle, and be your authentic self. You will be amazed at the unexpected good things that come into your life when you make the most of these "boondoggles".**

IT IS THE COMPANY THAT YOU KEEP

Successful fashion people create circles of friends within the industry--- but also always from the art world, design, technology, journalism, education, medicine, media, philanthropy, finance, etc. The most interesting people do not surround themselves with people who all think alike, work in the same industry, live in the same town or city, belong to the same political party, etc. Instead, they collect, and cultivate individual friendships very proactively.

Celebrate the differences among us and become the fabric that brings together people, ideas, religions, cultures, and individual lifestyles. Inspiration never comes from sameness.

The Lesson: Follow this model.

DOING GOOD IS GOOD BUSINESS

Anna is exceptionally philanthropically minded. Celebrated in terribly so-phisticated circles as a formidable fundraiser, Anna Wintour has in her own right raised goodness only knows how many millions of dollars to benefit organizations in the arts, education, and more.

But what you might not know is that *Vogue* itself has also raised untold millions over the years, and for a very long list of causes.

For example, a fledgling Dress for Success turned to *Vogue* for support. The magazine immediately generated clothing and financial donations at reader events, and showcased Dress for Success in its press releases to spotlight this important partnership. *Vogue* has given literally countless other organizations an enormous leg up.

But it did not stop there. Every month, *Vogue* planned, paid for, and executed events it hosted all over the U.S. to which it invited its readers to meet someone interesting, perhaps take in a *Vogue* hosted fashion show, and shop. The setting for these events was always an advertiser's store.

The magazine held these individual events multiple times a week, month after month, year after year. Its objective was to drive in-store sales to maxi-mum effect on the day, and generate profits for its advertising partners.

Important to note is that *Vogue* required of each advertiser for whom it hosted one of these events, a donation of a minimum of fifteen percent of the event's sales to a charity of *Vogue's* choice. Susan G. Komen and Best Buddies are two examples of the many organizations selected to benefit.

Vogue was keenly aware of its ability to drive profits for its partners, and used its power to fill the coffers of charitable entities it admired. Those who fail to see *Vogue* as a philanthropic force are missing a critical compo-nent of this big picture.

The Lesson: The most successful organizations think outside themselves. Standard operating procedure at *Vogue* required a philanthropic contribution as part

of any for-profit execution. Look for opportunities to follow *Vogue's* model in your own career.

WORK HARDER THAN THE NEXT GUY

People who are successful work very hard, often 12-14 hours a day.

The Lesson: Arrive early to the office, and leave late. Especially when starting any new job.

NEVER BURN YOUR BRIDGES

Do your best to stay on good terms with past employers, and former colleagues. This is not always possible of course, but make every attempt to do so.

The Lesson: You should do this for the right reasons. But you will also be surprised at the extent to which people from your past will pop up in future phases of your life.

CULTIVATE A HIGHLY IRREVERENT SENSE OF HUMOR: YOU WILL NEED ONE

Give yourself permission to develop a tongue-in-cheek sense of humor, and an appreciation for the absurd.

At *Vogue*, we laughed a lot. Strictly behind closed doors, we often thumbed our noses at that which was going on around us. The material we witnessed daily was stuff that no one could possibly make up, and some of it even ended up in the movies.

The Lesson: Everyday, we relied on laughter to shake off the stress, and regroup. It reminded us to look on the bright side, and enjoy the wild --- and most likely temporary ride --- that was our life at ***Vogue.***

#24: *EVERYTHING I NEED TO KNOW I LEARNED AT VOGUE*
Maria Devaney, Georgetown '90, would like to thank fellow alum Condé Montrose Nast, Georgetown Class of 1894, without whom this book could not have been written.

Maria would also like to thank Franny Nast, Condé Nast's aunt, for funding her nephew's education since his parents were financially unable to do so.

After graduating from Georgetown University, Condé Nast went into magazine publishing with a college classmate. Condé broke off on his own in 1909 to acquire an obscure society magazine called Vogue. Condé Nast singlehandedly turned it into the Vogue we now know, and went on to build around it the modern global media empire that is today his namesake.

"Everything I Need to Know I Learned at Vogue" began as a private letter to the author's then seven-year-old daughter Margaux, but evolved into a three-year on-campus workshop for students of The Georgetown Scholarship Program.

A percentage of the proceeds from this project will be donated to The Georgetown Scholarship Program.

Maria Devaney spent fourteen years working in fashion and media at Bergdorf Goodman, *Vogue*, and *The New York Times*.

Maria graduated from Georgetown University, and lives in the New York Metropolitan area with her husband and three children.

Acknowledgments: For editorial collaboration, to Michele Matrisciani of Bookchic LLC, www.bookchic.net.

29042818R00049

Made in the USA
San Bernardino, CA
11 March 2019